Because Is Awesome!

Discovering How Amazing He Really Is

Brad & Kathy Bright

Matt. 19:14 ♡

Brad and Kathy Bright

Adapted from Bill Bright's
GOD: Discover His Character

Illustrated by Lori Day

HARVEST HOUSE PUBLISHERS
EUGENE, OREGON

We dedicate this book to our father and father-in-love, Bill Bright. He taught and lived the simple wisdom contained in these pages and accomplished what few men have even dared to attempt. We have adapted that life-empowering message for children of all ages. Thank you, Dad, for giving us the most important gift one can give—a deep understanding of who God really is and why it matters.

Brad and Kathy Bright

Because God Is Awesome!

Text copyright © 2013 by Bright Media Foundation
Artwork copyright © Bright Media Foundation

Published by Harvest House Publishers
Eugene, Oregon 97402
www.harvesthousepublishers.com

ISBN 978-0-7369-5406-8

Design and production by Mary pat Design, Westport, Connecticut

Adapted from Bill Bright's *GOD: Discover His Character,*
copyright © 2002, Bright Media Foundation, Orlando, Florida

The *Discover God Study Bible* is an edition of the *Holy Bible,* New Living Translation. Scripture quotations are taken from the *Holy Bible,* New Living Translation, copyright © 1996, 2004. Used by permission of Tyndale House Publishers, Inc., Carol Stream, Illinois 60189.
All rights reserved.

Printed in China

13 14 15 16 17 18 19 20 21 / RDS / 10 9 8 7 6 5 4 3 2 1

CONTENTS

Dear friends,

When our first child was born, we felt totally unprepared for the responsibility. How could we teach the bundle in our arms all he would need to know to be successful in life? Brad's dad, Bill Bright, encouraged us with these words: "The most important thing to teach another [person] is who God is." He believed this to be true for his grandchildren as well.

Why did the man who wrote *The Four Spiritual Laws* (more than 2.5 billion printed) and founded the largest ministry organization in history long for his grandchildren to know the character of God above all else? He knew what many of us had forgotten: "Everything about our lives...is influenced by our view of God." He went on to say, "We can trace all our human problems to our view

of God." How our children view God will determine whether they see the challenges of life as problems or embrace them as opportunities to see their all-powerful, loving, sovereign God work.

If you want children to have strength when they feel powerless and comfort when their hearts are broken, teach them who God really is. If you want them to have courage to face their "giants" and compassion to help those in need, teach them who God really is. If you want them to pursue justice, extend mercy, choose truth, and cultivate integrity, read this book with them and begin laying the only foundation that will never fail them!

For His children's sake,

Brad and Kathy Bright

HOW TO USE THIS BOOK

This book is easy and fun to use! Although God has many attributes, we are highlighting just thirteen of them. We've arranged the "Because God is..." statements in triplets. Your children will learn about the attribute, why it matters to them, and how it can help them help others.

Try reading one "Because God is..." statement each night, and be sure to reserve some time to use the conversation starter to talk about it.

CONVERSATION STARTERS

The conversation starters will launch you into amazing dialogues with your kids! You will learn things about them you may not discover otherwise. The key is to have a few follow-up questions ready to prime the pump. For example, here is a conversation a friend had with his six-year-old son.

SON: "DAD, DID YOU KNOW THAT ADAM AND EVE WERE POOR?"

DAD: "NO. WHY WERE THEY POOR?"

SON: "THEY HAD NO MONEY TO BUY ANYTHING, EVEN CLOTHES."

"Why" is a great question to have in your tool kit. We miss opportunities to discover the how and why behind a child's thinking when we are too quick to correct and too slow to listen.

Here are some other follow-up questions.

7

- **HOW DOES THAT MAKE YOU FEEL?**

- **HOW DO YOU THINK THAT MAKES GOD FEEL?**

- **HAVE YOU HEARD SOMETHING DIFFERENT THAN THIS? HAVE FRIENDS, TEACHERS, OR SOMEONE ON TV SAID SOMETHING ELSE? IF SO, WHAT HAVE YOU HEARD?**

Finally, be prepared to answer the conversation starters too. Your experiences, thoughts, and feelings will help your children share their own thoughts, experiences, and feelings.

WHAT IF I DON'T KNOW THE ANSWERS?

If you're like us, your child will occasionally ask questions you don't know how to answer. We usually respond like this:

> **"THAT'S A GREAT QUESTION! I DON'T KNOW THE ANSWER RIGHT NOW, BUT I'LL FIND THE ANSWER, AND WE'LL TALK ABOUT IT AGAIN."**

It's okay for kids to see that we don't have all the answers.

Feel free to email us at info@dg4kids.com if you need help finding answers to your child's questions.

A REMINDER

Some attributes of God are more popular than others. God's love gets a lot of attention, while His justice is often ignored. How many sermons, if any, on God's justice have you heard? The result of this potluck approach to God is that many are embracing a false god, and they don't even know it.

All of God's attributes work together to make Him the only true God. Ignoring or minimizing even one attribute has a catastrophic domino effect on all His other attributes. For example, because God is holy, He is perfect and clean in every way. It is His holiness that makes His love perfect. Because God is holy, His love is never warped, abusive, or aloof. If He weren't holy, His love would be flawed, and at best it would become just another form of tolerance.

DON'T SKIP OVER ANY OF GOD'S
ATTRIBUTES. CHILDREN NEED TO LEARN
ABOUT ALL OF THEM AND HOW THEY
WORK SO PERFECTLY TOGETHER.
WHEN IT COMES TO GOD'S CHARACTER,
IT'S ALL OR NOTHING.

Because God Is PERSONAL...

Because God is personal,
you can get to know Him better every day.

[Jesus said,] "I am the good shepherd; I know My own sheep, and they know Me."
John 10:14

CONVERSATION STARTER

WHO IS YOUR CLOSEST FRIEND?

WHAT DO YOU LIKE TO DO WITH YOUR FRIENDS?

HOW DO YOU GET TO KNOW SOMEONE BETTER? DO YOU TALK WITH THEM? LISTEN TO THEM? DO THINGS WITH THEM?

It's the same with God! You can talk with Him by praying, listen to Him by reading the Bible, and hang out at His house by going to church. You can talk with others who know Him too.

HOW DO YOU THINK IT MAKES GOD FEEL WHEN YOU REMEMBER TO TALK WITH HIM EVERY DAY?

Because God is personal,
you can talk with Him about anything and everything.

Don't worry about anything; instead, pray about everything. Tell God what you need, and thank Him for all He has done. Then you will experience God's peace, which exceeds anything we can understand. His peace will guard your hearts and minds as you live in Christ Jesus. Philippians 4:6-7

CONVERSATION STARTER

God cares about you when you're sad and laughs with you when you're happy. You can tell Him anything!

IF YOU COULD SEE JESUS SITTING HERE RIGHT NOW, WHAT WOULD YOU WANT TO TALK ABOUT OR ASK HIM?

Because God is personal,
He helps you to be a good friend to others.

Don't look out only for your own interests, but take an interest in others, too.
Philippians 2:4

CONVERSATION STARTER

Jesus (God's only Son) died on the cross to pay the penalty for our sin. That's amazing friendship and love!

YOU DON'T HAVE TO DIE FOR YOUR FRIENDS LIKE JESUS DID, BUT WHAT *CAN* YOU DO TO BE A GOOD FRIEND?

Because God Is ALL-POWERFUL...

Because God is all-powerful,
there is nothing bigger or stronger than God.

O Sovereign LORD! You made the heavens and earth by Your strong hand and powerful arm. Nothing is too hard for You! Jeremiah 32:17

Conversation Starter

WHO ARE YOUR FAVORITE SUPERHEROES?

WHY?

Every superhero has a weakness. Only God is all-powerful. He doesn't have any weaknesses.

AREN'T YOU GLAD GOD DOESN'T HAVE *ANY* WEAKNESSES? Nothing is too hard for Him!

Because God is all-powerful,

when He becomes your friend, *nothing* can ever separate you from His love.

And I am convinced that nothing can ever separate us from God's love. Neither death nor life, neither angels nor demons, neither our fears for today nor our worries about tomorrow—not even the powers of hell can separate us from God's love. No power in the sky above or in the earth below—indeed, nothing in all creation will ever be able to separate us from the love of God that is revealed in Christ Jesus our Lord.

Romans 8:38-39

CONVERSATION STARTER

CAN YOU THINK OF SOMETHING THAT'S VERY HARD FOR YOU TO DO? WHAT IS IT?

Maybe being nice to a brother or sister, finishing your chores, or doing better in school is hard for you.

WHAT DO YOU WANT TO ASK GOD TO HELP YOU WITH THIS WEEK?

Because God is all-powerful,

He is strong enough to help you with anything.

For I can do everything through Christ, who gives me strength.
Philippians 4:13

CONVERSATION STARTER

WHAT CAN KEEP YOU AWAY FROM THE PEOPLE YOU LOVE?

DOES MOVING TO ANOTHER CITY?

WHAT IF SOMEONE DIES?

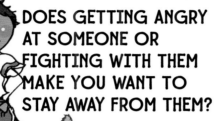

DOES GETTING ANGRY AT SOMEONE OR FIGHTING WITH THEM MAKE YOU WANT TO STAY AWAY FROM THEM?

God promises that He will always be with you and that *nothing* is strong enough to keep you away from Him once you accept Jesus' payment for your sin.

HOW DO YOU KNOW THAT GOD IS YOUR FRIEND?

(If you're not sure, go to the 4 Keys 4Kids section on page 90.)

Because God Is HOLY...

Because God is holy,
He is perfect and clean in every way!

Holy, holy, holy is the Lord God, the Almighty—the one who always was, who is, and who is still to come.
Revelation 4:8

He is the Rock; His deeds are perfect. Everything He does is just and fair. He is a faithful God who does no wrong; how just and upright He is!
Deuteronomy 32:4

CONVERSATION STARTER

It's God's holiness that makes all His other attributes perfect. Because God is holy, His love is perfect and pure. He always uses His power for good. He is always fair. He always tells the truth. God's holiness makes everything about God perfect!

WHAT DO YOU LIKE BEST ABOUT GOD?

IS IT HIS LOVE, HIS POWER, OR MAYBE THE FACT THAT HE'S EVERYWHERE ALL THE TIME?

WHY DO YOU LIKE IT BEST?

Because God is holy, you can count on Him to be perfect all the time and in every way!

Because God is holy (perfect and clean),

He is able to make your sinful heart clean.

Fighting

Mean Thoughts

Lying

Arguing

Disobeying

If we confess our sins to Him, He is faithful and just to forgive us our sins and to cleanse us from all wickedness.
1 John 1:9

CONVERSATION STARTER

Sin is anything we do, say, or even think that isn't totally perfect and clean. It's like saying "no" to God and His Word.

DO YOU THINK IT MAKES GOD FEEL HAPPY OR SAD WHEN YOU SAY "NO" TO HIM?

DO YOU KNOW ANYONE, OTHER THAN GOD, WHO'S PERFECT ALL THE TIME?

WHEN YOU SIN, HOW CAN YOUR HEART BECOME CLEAN AGAIN?

(For help, read the 4 Keys 4Kids section on page 90.)

Because God is holy (perfect and clean),

He helps you be a light for Him and say "no" to sin.

For once you were full of darkness, but now you have light from the Lord. So live as people of light! For this light within you produces only what is good and right and true.
Ephesians 5:8-9

CONVERSATION STARTER

 ARE YOU BEING A LIGHT WHEN YOU LIE?

 ARE YOU BEING A LIGHT WHEN YOU'RE MEAN?

 ARE YOU BEING A LIGHT WHEN YOU FORGIVE OTHERS LIKE JESUS DID?

HOW WERE YOU A LIGHT TODAY?

Let God's light shine in you!

Because God Is LOVE...

Because God is love,

He loves you very much and wants you to know Him.

For God loved the world so much that He gave His one and only Son [Jesus], so that everyone who believes in Him will not perish but have eternal life.   John 3:16

Conversation Starter

HOW DO YOU SHOW OTHER PEOPLE YOU LOVE THEM?

DO YOU GIVE THEM HUGS, KISSES, AND PRESENTS?

DO YOU SPEND TIME WITH THEM AND HELP THEM WITHOUT BEING ASKED?

God loves us so much that He sent His only Son to die for our sins! Now that's amazing love!

HOW CAN YOU SHOW GOD YOU LOVE HIM?

Because God is love,

He only does what is best for you.

We know how much God loves us, and we have put our trust in His love.
1 John 4:16

There is no greater love than to lay down one's life for one's friends. You are My friends if you do what I command.
John 15:13-14

CONVERSATION STARTER

Tell about a time when you wanted to do something dangerous—like running into the street without looking both ways for cars—and someone stopped you.

DID YOU GET IN TROUBLE?

WHY DO YOU THINK THAT PERSON STOPPED YOU?

DO YOU THINK THAT PERSON STOPPED YOU BECAUSE THEY LOVED YOU OR BECAUSE THEY WANTED TO BE MEAN?

God loves you so much that He doesn't want you to do things that will harm you or your friendship with Him. Sometimes He says "no" to things we want because He knows it's not the best for us. The Ten Commandments are His rules for a joy-filled life. Following His commands will keep us close to God and His love.

Because God is love,
He will help you love others!

Dear friends, let us continue to love one another, for love comes from God. Anyone who loves is a child of God and knows God. But anyone who does not love does not know God, for God is love.

1 John 4:7-8

CONVERSATION STARTER

OF THE PEOPLE YOU KNOW, WHO IS EASY TO LOVE? WHY?

WHO IS HARD TO LOVE? WHY?

God loves everyone! Jesus even loved the men who nailed Him to the cross. It's hard for us to love people who aren't nice, but God says He will help us.

HOW DO YOU THINK IT MAKES GOD FEEL WHEN YOU LOVE OTHERS?

WHO DO YOU NEED GOD'S HELP TO LOVE?

HOW CAN YOU SHOW GOD'S LOVE TO SOMEONE THIS WEEK?

Because God Is EVERYWHERE...

Because God is everywhere,
He is always with you!
You are never alone!

I can never escape from Your Spirit! I can never get away from Your presence! If I go up to heaven, You are there; if I go down to the grave, You are there. If I ride the wings of the morning, if I dwell by the farthest oceans, even there Your hand will guide me, and Your strength will support me.

Psalm 139:7-10

Conversation Starter
WHAT WAS YOUR FAVORITE PART OF TODAY?

God was with you every minute of the day.

WHAT DO YOU THINK WAS HIS FAVORITE PART OF THE DAY? WHY?

Because God is everywhere, He is with you even when you feel alone.

WHAT DO YOU THINK ABOUT THAT?

Because God is everywhere,

He sees everything you do—the good and the bad, even when no one else is around!

The LORD is watching everywhere, keeping His eye on both the evil and the good.
Proverbs 15:3

CONVERSATION STARTER

IF PEOPLE COULD SEE GOD BESIDE THEM ALL THE TIME, DO YOU THINK IT WOULD MAKE A DIFFERENCE IN WHAT THEY DO AND SAY?

WOULD IT MAKE A DIFFERENCE IN WHAT YOU DO AND SAY? WHY?

HOW DO YOU THINK GOD FEELS WHEN YOU TRY TO BE GOOD?

Because God is everywhere,

you can stand up for what is right because you know He is with you.

This is My command—be strong and courageous!
Do not be afraid or discouraged. For the LORD your
God is with you wherever you go.   Joshua 1:9

CONVERSATION STARTER

Standing up for what is right can be hard, especially if no one else is doing it with you!

HAVE YOU EVER HAD TO STAND UP FOR WHAT'S RIGHT, LIKE TELLING THE TRUTH WHEN ALL YOUR FRIENDS ARE LYING OR BEING NICE TO SOMEONE WHEN EVERYONE ELSE IS BEING MEAN TO THEM?

God is always with you, and He promises to never leave you so you can stand strong!

HOW DO YOU THINK IT MAKES GOD FEEL WHEN YOU STAND UP FOR WHAT IS RIGHT?

Because God Is
TOTALLY TRUTHFUL...

Because God is totally truthful,
what He says in the Bible is true.
It is your compass for life!

Every word of God proves true.
Proverbs 30:5

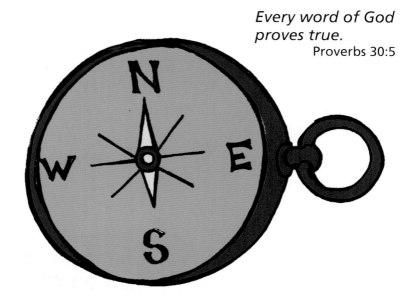

CONVERSATION STARTER

HAVE YOU EVER BEEN TOLD SOMETHING THAT TURNED OUT TO BE UNTRUE?

Sometimes you may hear something on the news or from teachers or read something in books that turns out to be false. Sometimes this happens by accident because they didn't have all the facts. However, everything God says in the Bible is totally true! God has all the facts all the time, so He never has to say oops!

IF YOU HEAR SOMETHING THAT IS DIFFERENT THAN WHAT GOD SAYS IN THE BIBLE, WHICH DO YOU THINK IS TRUE?

Because God is totally truthful,
He will never lie to you.

God is not a man, so He does not lie. He is not human, so He does not change His mind.
Numbers 23:19

CONVERSATION STARTER

God cannot lie.

CAN YOU IMAGINE *NEVER* TELLING A LIE—NOT EVEN A LITTLE WHITE LIE OR A FIB? WHY DO PEOPLE SOMETIMES LIE?

God *always* tells the truth. You can count on Him to always be honest.

HOW DOES THAT MAKE YOU FEEL ABOUT HIM?

Because God is totally truthful,
He will help you tell the truth.

Don't lie to each other, for you have stripped off your old sinful nature and all its wicked deeds. Put on your new nature, and be renewed as you learn to know your Creator and become like Him.
Colossians 3:9-10

Truthful

Honest

Sincere

Faithful

Trustworthy

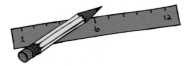

The LORD detests lying lips, but He delights in those who tell the truth.
Proverbs 12:22

CONVERSATION STARTER

IS IT HARD FOR YOU TO TELL THE TRUTH ALL THE TIME?

WHY?

God promises to help you! Next time you're about to tell a lie, stop, take two breaths, and ask God to help you tell the truth.

Because God Is MERCIFUL...

Because God is merciful,
His Son, Jesus, paid the price for
your sins so you wouldn't have to.

*For everyone has sinned; we
all fall short of God's glorious
standard [perfection].*
Romans 3:23

*But God showed His great love for
us by sending Christ [Jesus] to die
for us while we were still sinners.*
Romans 5:8

CONVERSATION STARTER

WHAT IS YOUR FAVORITE TOY? Imagine someone broke it.

HOW WOULD YOU FEEL?

WHAT SHOULD THE PERSON DO ABOUT IT?
PAY FOR IT?
FIX IT?
DO NOTHING?

Mercy means you don't make them pay the price.

WHEN YOU ARE MERCIFUL, WHO PAYS THE PRICE?

You do. You either have to buy a new toy or go without one. Mercy always has a price.

Sin has a price too. Jesus died a horrible death to pay for our sins. When we accept Jesus' payment for our sins, we don't have to pay the price ourselves. That's amazing love and mercy!

Because God is merciful,

He forgives you when you ask in
Jesus' name and really mean it.

*For the wages [payment] of
sin is death, but the free gift
of God is eternal life through
Christ Jesus our Lord.*
Romans 6:23

CONVERSATION STARTER

WHAT IS THE BEST PRESENT YOU EVER RECEIVED? WHY WAS IT THE BEST?

Pretend the gift is still wrapped and sitting in the room unopened.

WOULD YOU BE ABLE TO PLAY WITH THE GIFT?

IF YOU'VE NEVER OPENED THE GIFT, IS IT DOING YOU ANY GOOD?

No! You have to accept the gift and open it or it does you no good. It's the same with God's mercy. Jesus died in your place, but you have to accept His gift of mercy to receive His forgiveness.

HAVE YOU ACCEPTED HIS GIFT?

Because God is merciful,

He wants you to be merciful to others.

God blesses those who are merciful, for they will be shown mercy.
Matthew 5:7

Helpful

Upset

Happy

Sad

CONVERSATION STARTER

WHO IS THE MEANEST PERSON YOU KNOW?

WHY DO YOU THINK THEY'RE MEAN?

Jesus says we are to show mercy to others the way He shows mercy to us. That doesn't mean we agree with their sin, but rather we show them Jesus' love in spite of their sin. Ask Him to help you show mercy and love even to mean, selfish people!

Mean

Forgiving

Encouraging

Angry

Because God KNOWS EVERYTHING...

Because God knows everything,
He knows *everything* about you!

"Can anyone hide from Me in a secret place? Am I not everywhere in all the heavens and earth?" says the LORD.
Jeremiah 23:24

Yes, I obey Your commandments and laws because You know everything I do.
Psalm 119:168

CONVERSATION STARTER

WHAT IS SOMETHING MOST OF YOUR FRIENDS DON'T KNOW ABOUT YOU?

IS THERE ANYTHING YOU DON'T WANT THEM TO KNOW ABOUT YOU?

God knows everything you do and everything you think. He understands you perfectly and loves you very much.

Because God knows everything,
you can go to Him with all your worries and questions.

In Him lie hidden all the treasures of wisdom and knowledge.
Colossians 2:3

If you need wisdom, ask our generous God, and He will give it to you. He will not rebuke you for asking.
James 1:5

CONVERSATION STARTER

WHAT QUESTION WOULD YOU LIKE TO ASK GOD?

ARE YOU WORRIED ABOUT ANYTHING RIGHT NOW?

You can be honest with Him about all your worries and questions because He knows it all anyway! He knows the answer to all your questions and will help you when you ask.

Because God knows everything,

He can show you how to help others.

So we have not stopped praying for you since we first heard about you. We ask God to give you complete knowledge of His will and to give you spiritual wisdom and understanding.

Colossians 1:9

CONVERSATION STARTER

HAVE YOU HELPED SOMEONE RECENTLY? HOW?

Sometimes it's hard to know how to help those around you, but God knows. He knows everything! Ask Him to show you how to help those who are hurting or in need. One way to help is to pray for others to know God.

WHO WOULD YOU LIKE TO PRAY FOR?

Because God Is
ALWAYS RIGHT...

Because God is always right,
He is never wrong! I can trust that
everything He says and does is right.

*O LORD, You are righteous, and Your regulations are
fair. Your laws are perfect and completely trustworthy.*
Psalm 119:137-138

CONVERSATION STARTER

HAVE YOU EVER SAID SOMETHING THAT TURNED OUT TO BE WRONG?

WHAT WAS IT?

DO YOU KNOW ANYONE WHO IS RIGHT *ALL* THE TIME?

Not even scientists are right all the time. In the 1970s scientists said the earth was getting colder and going into another ice age. Obviously that didn't happen! They were wrong because they didn't have all the information they needed to have the right answer. God knows *everything*, He's *everywhere*, He's *all-powerful*, and He's *totally truthful*. He existed even before the universe was created! Put those facts together, and it's impossible for God to be wrong!

Because God is always right,
He knows what's best for you!

The commandments of the LORD are right, bringing joy to the heart. The commands of the LORD are clear, giving insight for living.
Psalm 19:8

Conversation Starter

WHAT ARE SOME OF THE RULES IN YOUR HOUSE? CAN YOU NAME SOME OF THE RULES GOD GAVE US IN THE BIBLE, SUCH AS ONE OR TWO OF THE TEN COMMANDMENTS?

Some people think that God's rules take the fun out of life, but it's really the other way around! God knows what is best, and His commandments show us how to have the best life possible.

WHICH ONE OF GOD'S COMMANDMENTS IS EASIEST FOR YOU TO FOLLOW? WHICH IS THE HARDEST?

Ask God to help you do what's right and follow His commandments every day.

1. Put God first and don't believe in any other god.
2. Don't love anything more than God and don't make idols.
3. Always use God's name with respect.
4. Keep the Sabbath a day for rest and church.
5. Honor your father and mother.
6. Do not murder.
7. Do not cheat on your husband or wife.
8. Do not steal.
9. Do not lie.
10. Do not wish for other people's things.

Because God is always right,
He will help you to do what's right.

I have hidden Your word in my heart,
that I might not sin against You.

Psalm 119:11

So I say, let the Holy Spirit guide your lives.
Then you won't be doing what your sinful nature
craves... But the Holy Spirit produces this kind
of fruit in our lives: love, joy, peace, patience,
kindness, goodness, faithfulness, gentleness, and
self-control. There is no law against these things!

Galatians 5:16,22-23

CONVERSATION STARTER

God can never be wrong—not even once.

IF SOMEONE SAYS SOMETHING DIFFERENT THAN WHAT GOD SAYS IN THE BIBLE, WHO IS RIGHT?

WHAT CAN YOU DO TODAY TO BEGIN LEARNING MORE ABOUT WHAT GOD SAYS?

Because God Is FAITHFUL...

Because God is faithful,
you can be sure He always keeps His promises!

O Lord God of Heaven's Armies! Where is there anyone as mighty as You, O Lord? You are entirely faithful.
Psalm 89:8

If we are unfaithful, He remains faithful, for He cannot deny who He is.
2 Timothy 2:13

CONVERSATION STARTER

HAS SOMEONE EVER BROKEN A PROMISE TO YOU?

HAVE YOU EVER BROKEN A PROMISE YOU MADE?

WHY IS IT HARD TO KEEP EACH AND EVERY ONE OF OUR PROMISES?

God made lots of amazing promises in the Bible, and He can keep each and every one of them! Not only *can* He keep His promises (He's all-powerful), He *will* keep His promises because it's in His nature to be faithful to His Word. God can't be unfaithful!

Because God is faithful,
you can trust He will do what He says, even if you don't see it right away.

*Understand, therefore, that the L*ORD *your God is indeed God. He is the faithful God who keeps His covenant for a thousand generations and lavishes His unfailing love on those who love Him and obey His commands.*

Deuteronomy 7:9

CONVERSATION STARTER

When Adam and Eve said "no" to God and disobeyed Him, God promised to send someone to pay for sin and make a way for us to be forgiven. That happened thousands of years before Jesus came to earth to keep God's promise. That's a long time! The Bible says God waited until the perfect time to send Jesus to earth. You can count on His promises coming true at just the right time because God is faithful!

HAVE YOU EVER HAD TO WAIT ON A PROMISE?

WHAT WAS THE PROMISE?

WAS IT HARD TO WAIT?

WAS IT WORTH THE WAIT?

Because God is faithful,
He helps you be faithful to Him and His Word (the Bible).

Don't be afraid, for I am with you. Don't be discouraged, for I am your God. I will strengthen you and help you. I will hold you up with My victorious right hand.

Isaiah 41:10

CONVERSATION STARTER

Being faithful to God isn't always easy. Sometimes it's hard to do what God wants us to do.

HOW DO YOU THINK IT MAKES GOD FEEL WHEN YOU ARE FAITHFUL TO HIM?

WHAT'S THE HARDEST THING FOR YOU TO DO FAITHFULLY?

IS IT HARD TO BE NICE TO A BROTHER OR SISTER, ALWAYS TELL THE TRUTH, LEARN BIBLE VERSES, KEEP YOUR ROOM CLEAN, REMEMBER TO TALK WITH GOD EVERY DAY, OR HELP SOMEONE WHO'S HURTING?

WHY IS IT HARD TO DO?

Ask God to help you be faithful to Him and His Word.

Because God Is the CREATOR AND KING...

Because God is the Creator and King,
He made everything and is in control of everything.

You rule the oceans. You subdue their storm-tossed waves. You crushed the great sea monster. You scattered Your enemies with Your mighty arm. The heavens are Yours, and the earth is Yours; everything in the world is Yours—You created it all.

Psalm 89:9-11

Conversation Starter

OF ALL THE THINGS THAT GOD CREATED, WHAT'S YOUR FAVORITE?

WHY?

HOW DO THINK GOD FELT WHEN HE CREATED YOU?

Because God is
the Creator and King,
no one can mess up His plan for you!

You can make many plans, but the LORD's purpose will prevail.
Proverbs 19:21

"For I know the plans I have for you," says the LORD. "They are plans for good and not for disaster, to give you a future and a hope."
Jeremiah 29:11

CONVERSATION STARTER

WHAT DO YOU WANT TO BE WHEN YOU GROW UP?

WHEN YOUR PARENTS WERE LITTLE, WHAT DID THEY WANT TO BE WHEN THEY GREW UP?

God is in control of your future, and He will make sure nothing ruins His plan. It doesn't mean everything will go the way you want it. God's plan allows us to make good and bad choices, but you can be sure that He will get you where you need to be in the end!

Because God is
the Creator and King,
you are His masterpiece, and
He made you to do good things.

For we are God's masterpiece. He has created us anew in Christ Jesus, so we can do the good things He planned for us long ago.

Ephesians 2:10

CONVERSATION STARTER

There has never been someone just like you! You are God's one-of-a-kind masterpiece!

HOW DO YOU THINK GOD FEELS ABOUT YOU?

WHAT ARE SOME THINGS YOU THINK HE CREATED YOU TO DO TO HELP OTHERS?

FOR EXAMPLE, DO YOU HAVE A KIND HEART TO HELP THOSE WHO ARE HURTING?

DID HE GIVE YOU STRONG MUSCLES TO HELP THOSE WHO NEED A HELPING HAND OR A SMART BRAIN TO HELP SOLVE PROBLEMS?

Thank God for creating you to do good things!

Because God Is JUST...

Because God is just,
He will always treat you fairly.

He is the Rock; His deeds are perfect. Everything He does is just and fair. He is a faithful God who does no wrong; how just and upright He is!
Deuteronomy 32:4

For the LORD is coming to judge the earth. He will judge the world with justice, and the nations with fairness.
Psalm 98:9

Conversation Starter

HAS SOMEONE EVER BLAMED YOU FOR SOMETHING YOU DIDN'T DO?

WERE YOU PUNISHED FOR IT?

HAVE YOU EVER DONE SOMETHING WRONG AND GOTTEN AWAY WITH IT?

Because God is everywhere, sees everything, and is just, He's the only one who always judges us fairly.

Because God is just,
someone has to pay the penalty for your sin.

For God loved the world so much that He gave His one and only Son, so that everyone who believes in Him will not perish but have eternal life. John 3:16

Jesus told him, "I am the way, the truth, and the life. No one can come to the Father except through Me." John 14:6

CONVERSATION STARTER

HAS SOMEONE EVER HURT YOU AND THEN NOT BEEN PUNISHED FOR IT?

HOW DID THAT MAKE YOU FEEL?

DO YOU THINK SIN MAKES GOD SAD?

WOULD GOD BE FAIR AND JUST IF HE DID NOT PUNISH ALL SIN?

AREN'T YOU GLAD JESUS DIED IN YOUR PLACE TO PAY THE PENALTY FOR YOUR SIN?

Try to remember to thank God every day for Jesus!

Because God is just,

He will help you stand up for what is right and fair!

*He loves whatever is just and good; the
unfailing love of the LORD fills the earth.*
Psalm 33:5

*This is what the LORD of Heaven's Armies says: Judge
fairly, and show mercy and kindness to one another.*
Zechariah 7:9

CONVERSATION STARTER

HAVE YOU EVER SEEN SOMEONE GET BULLIED OR TREATED UNFAIRLY?

DID YOU TRY TO HELP OR GO TO GET HELP?

Not only does God want us to treat others fairly, but He wants us to help others when they are mistreated.

Because God
NEVER CHANGES...

Because God never changes,
His character never changes!

I am the LORD, and I do not change.
Malachi 3:6

CONVERSATION STARTER

 **WHAT DO YOU LIKE MOST ABOUT GOD?**

 **WHAT IF GOD'S LOVE CHANGED?**

 **WHAT IF GOD'S POWER CHANGED?**

 **WHAT IF HIS HOLINESS CHANGED?**

 **AREN'T YOU GLAD THAT GOD *NEVER* CHANGES?**

Our personal Creator and King is always the same. You can depend on His love, power, faithfulness, mercy, justice, presence, knowledge, righteousness, holiness, and truthfulness to be the same today and in the future just as they were in Bible times!

Because God never changes,
you never have to worry about the future!

Jesus Christ is the same
yesterday, today, and forever.
Hebrews 13:8

Whatever is good and perfect comes down to us
from God our Father, who created all the lights
in the heavens. He never changes or casts a
shifting shadow.

James 1:17

CONVERSATION STARTER

Not all change is bad.

HOW HAVE YOU CHANGED IN THE LAST YEAR?

WHAT CAN YOU DO NOW THAT YOU COULDN'T DO LAST YEAR?

CAN YOU NOW RIDE A BIKE, READ A STORY, OR RUN MUCH FASTER?

Some change is good, and some change isn't. However, because God is already perfect, He doesn't change. No matter what change happens in your life, you can be sure that God is always with you and that He's always the same.

HOW DOES THAT MAKE YOU FEEL?

Because God never changes,

He can help you just like
He helped the heroes in the Bible!

God is not a man, so He does not lie. He is not human, so He does not change His mind. Has He ever spoken and failed to act? Has He ever promised and not carried it through?
Numbers 23:19

CONVERSATION STARTER

WHO'S YOUR FAVORITE HERO IN THE BIBLE?

IS IT NOAH, MOSES, DAVID, QUEEN ESTHER, OR DANIEL?

WHY?

God made them heroes because they trusted Him. He said He would help them, and He did. Because God never changes, He will give you the strength to do what He asks you to do just like He gave strength to the heroes of the Bible!

4Keys 4Kids

1 GOD LOVES YOU!

Because God is love, He loves you very much and wants you to know Him.

For God loved the world so much that He gave His one and only Son [Jesus], so that everyone who believes in Him will not perish but have eternal life. John 3:16

You are God's special creation, and He has an amazing plan for you! God's plan starts with you getting to know Him.

And this is the way to have eternal life—to know You, the only true God, and Jesus Christ, the one You sent to earth. John 17:3

BUT THERE'S A PROBLEM...

SIN KEEPS US FROM GOD!

Because God is perfect (holy), everything He says, does, or thinks is totally good and right. Sin is anything we do, say, or even think that isn't totally good and right. It's like saying "no" to God.

For everyone has sinned; we all fall short of God's glorious standard.
Romans 3:23

We are all separated from God because of our sin. Sin is like a huge canyon that separates us from God. No matter how hard we try, we can never be good enough to reach God on our own.

For the wages [payment] of sin is death, but the free gift of God is eternal life through Christ Jesus our Lord.

Romans 6:23

WE CAN'T FIX OUR SIN PROBLEM, BUT GOD CAN!

③ ONLY JESUS CAN FIX OUR SIN PROBLEM!

Because God is merciful, He sent Jesus to fix our sin problem.

Christ [Jesus] died for our sins, just as the Scriptures said. He was buried, and He was raised from the dead on the third day, just as the Scriptures said. 1 Corinthians 15:3-4

That's why Jesus is the *only* way to God!

Jesus says in the Bible: "I am the way, the truth, and the life. No one can come to the Father except through Me." John 14:6

THERE IS SOMETHING EACH OF US MUST DO TO CROSS THE BRIDGE...

YOU MUST SAY "YES" TO JESUS!

Because God is personal, each of us must accept Jesus as our Savior and King.

What life do you want?

APART FROM GOD,
life is full of our...

Worry

Anger

Jealousy

Fear

Doubt

WITH GOD,
life is full of God's...

Love

Peace

Power

Joy

Security

Presence

If you want to know God, you must trust and accept Jesus. No one can do it for you. Only *you* can ask Jesus to forgive your sin. The Bible says: *"But to all who believed Him and accepted Him, He gave the right to become children of God"* (John 1:12). Do you believe that Jesus paid the penalty for your sin? Do you want a relationship with Him now and forever? If you said "yes," God's heart is bursting with joy!

SO WHAT'S NEXT?

HOW DO YOU ACCEPT JESUS' GIFT?

If you **BELIEVE** that Jesus is God's only Son and that He died for your sin and rose from the dead, all you have to do is:

- Tell Him you're **SORRY** for your sin.
- **ASK** Him to help you change.
- **ACCEPT** His gift of forgiveness.
- **ASK** Him to be your Savior and King!

YOU CAN ACCEPT JESUS' GIFT RIGHT NOW BY SHOWING YOUR TRUST THROUGH PRAYER.